I'LL BE YOUR MANIC ANXIETY QUEEN

POEMS

J. R. ROGUE

J.R. Rogue
PO Box 984
Lebanon, MO 65536
www.jrrogue.com
contact@jrrogue.com

CONTENTS

For all the mad, mad, people

CONTENT WARNINGS:

depression, anxiety, mania, agoraphobia, death, suicide

HOT FREEWAY

we war with dirty dishes,

with the unswept floor

with the way our ambitions

leave us wanting each other

we war in silent shades,

voices we will not raise

you know I am a deer

on the edge of your woods—

I'll run into a hot freeway

to escape a deep booming,

secrets on eruption

you know I will war with myself

if it means keeping you

you know I will retreat

to the far spaces,

& you won't

look for me there

MORE LOVER THAN YOU

I live in spaces between,

where *hellos* fade

into pillows,

where I wonder

If I am daydreaming

our love instead of living it

do we know

each other anymore?

night owl, & late night secrets

we pass in mornings,

kiss goodbye,

& I am drugged more

often than not,

surviving my brain

& the manic anxiety

that is more lover than you,

more vicious than you

you are calm waters,

silent strength

& hard-headed

insecurity

we love in spaces

in between,

& no one

can survive that

LONE HUMAN

do you hear my tears?

the fast-moving world,
the addictive chaos
you cling to—

it's falling away
everything quiets

the melancholy finally
not looking in
from the edge of the world

halted race,
you don't remember
my trailing

lone human, yes

& you hear my tears

but won't

shed your own

PULL ME UNDER

the loneliness is gripping

at times—

bright walls

& the sun speaking to me,

but you're not speaking to me

& that blessing burns

brilliant when I reach,

begging for crumbs

but you find white noise

& the company of

strangers a stronger pull

I am spare parts,

the sum of this

change in my pockets

my accomplishments

ring hollow to you,

even as pride

blooms in my chest

the loneliness is gripping

at times, & I wonder

when it will pull me

under again

I'm not a (your) princess,
but I'll be the queen of
the dramatic scenes you
play out in your head
when you hatch escape plans
knowing you don't have
it in you to
ever quit me

PAPER SMILES

right now,

I am surrounded

by paper smiles

& happy eyes

yet I can't get my own

to stick

around

for a while

my legs are heavy

& my fingers

useless

except at tapping

out my own

hollow

hell

THE NIGHT & THE TUMBLE

round & round

do I have a handle on this?

I'm off balance & bewildered

the streets are empty,

but my god

the birds are singing

I'm in the shower

counting water drops

& money dips

when was the last

time I felt like this?

when does the throbbing end?

dull ache

whispering want

round & round

I'm the dark & the jogger

the night & the tumble

the streets feel empty,

but my mind is leaking

THRONE-LESS

coffee stains on the blanket,

cat face close to mine,

slow yawn

I draw the blinds,

caress spite like a love,

kiss the dark like a funeral

there is a

hum outside,

a life unbridled,

I cannot break it

I haven't had a

new friend in years,

there isn't much to bend,

to break open to the microscope

I am burrowing

deep like a cockroach,

their legs can't

go backward

& I can't go

back to the days

they crawled

over skin like whispers

coffee stains

like a lover on my lips

bitter like a cold brew,

sweet like your eyes

when they wrinkle

I am your queen,

you are throne-less

as we shake

with the waking

of our promises

I HAVE A POEM IN MY HEAD

vile & unlike you,

soft in the center,

free for a laugh

& a hand that helps

the poem is acid,

heavy like the stones you place

on my back

I have a poem in my throat,

& I open wide,

offer you pennies & blood

soft of center,

high in morals,

a crown that doesn't fit,

but you don't mind the dent,

the hollow skull

& open mouth full of worship

I have a poem in my head,
& dreams of
you I wish away
on mornings filled
with the haze you leave behind

MY SAFE PLACE, MY POISON

& what if the world

fears what I crave?

time

& overrun faces cannot get me

their voices will not pull me

as I stay behind

brick & wall

& iron & glass

this home is a vengeful thief

a soundproof lover

& I worry I will fall deeper

this is my safe place

my poison

this is my warm hearth,

pyre prison

even when you

say it is the poison,

I drink heartily

agoraphobia, my lost lover

you are the knife

& I invite the blade

it is a terrible
thing living
inside
this mind

ALL THIS MOTHERING

I want to know you

can live for yourself

that all the happy you feel

can be grown of

your own heart,

that I will not have

to birth it

I have a black thumb

& a black center

I cannot be all this mothering,

this soft place

this love

you crave—

so ugly

& wanting,

so needy

I want to know you

can live for yourself,

so I can, too

THEY DON'T KNOW US

though they want to

they don't know
our secrets,
the trials,
the miles we have
walked to have this—
this thing that endures,
breathes deep,
lives through the salt

they don't
know our love,
the lingering
between our lips

it is ours alone,
& every inch

of each other's flesh

we have fought for

is worth it

I will not offer

my heart to another

I will not fight

for the love of another,

as long as you reach for me

they don't know us—

the miles we have walked

to have forever with

each other

MAD MAD LOVE

do you know what the taste

of my pulse tells?

do you know the red,

the humming,

the way I shiver in the

daylight as voices crescendo?

I am needing you—

calm waters,

protector of the

many faces I wear

I gave up the liquor,

gave into the shelter

of our haven,

& you long to live out loud,

I long to be the hush,

the whisper that lingers in the

mind of those with half

a mind to listen

to soft revelations

why do the buzzards

hover you?

why do the animals

peer in at night,

wondering at the workings

of our mad mad love?

do they know the red?

they think they do,

dissect the mirror,

the way we spill

all over each other

their imaginations

cannot fathom it,

our coupling

but we are a decade

above water,

above drowning

do you know

what the taste

of my pulse tells?

only you do

THIS HAUNTING FALL

I am falling

endless cavern

black eyes

wild worry

black guilt

taking root in my chest

an anchor

to the unknown

the middle space

the dirt & ebony

caress my eyes

I feel nothing

suspended & alone

I am falling

the bottom is you,

my best friend,

these children

it is a safe space

but still, each night

the fall

the endless cavern

the lingering

the festering ache

in the dark

the ebony caress

I am alive—

am I allowed this haunting fall?

THE KING OF THIS MAD LAND

I can smell your

obsession for me

some earthy thing,

ripping from your pores

like a demon

too long dwelling in the

caverns of this earth,

in the caverns of my

maddening mind

you crumpled my poems up

& shoved them down

your hungry throat

there's ink on your bottom lip

& I want to kiss it away

I can't figure out if

you're brave or mad

I can't figure out if

I want either in

my manic life

do you want to be

the king of this mad land?

I was always looking
for an escape

vices never changed
for me

CANNOT THAW

that same tire is leaking air,

the morning holds a violent chill,

& I hold a curse

where does the worry go

when I open my eyes?

pressed lips

shaking hands

the oil needs to be changed,

the kids need to be fed

I'm leaking air

falling into bed

too early, too often

who saves us from

this everyday life?

I am so very heavy

with this weight

on my shoulders,

in my heart

my poet's tongue

will speak this violent chill

this ice inside,

this yawn of dawn

it cannot thaw

FOR SCRAPS

tan tank top,

black thing,

your hand is soft—

soft pinch, handful of me,

& you are insatiable

I am warm & falling

Into the medicine,

the voices fall away,

& we are not like this enough

I miss you, your body,

the reminder of our first time

your calm is edible,

a drug all its own

I have been surviving

off of your afterglow for years,

warring with your walls just as many

tan tank top, hanging a little lower

than the day we met

no one questions

why we have lasted this long,

not those who know us

those who are waiting

for scraps,

pull out the microscope

you are insatiable,

& I am a ghost

I want you to resurrect me

RED MISTRESS

I remember walking

from room

to room—

a lipstick stain placed

just so on my wrist

I was my own red mistress

& you throwing

open the windows

as the train

cried by

where plastic

eyes tried

to make up

new lies to dance

in time with the

ones we held

too close

THIS FEVER DREAM OF A GIRL

leave here, go west

it tells me to flee,

this voice inside—

this gentle rumbling

leave family behind,

they're better off without

this warring shadow—

this fever dream of a girl

who snatches smiles from faces,

drowns hope in shallow graves

leave here, go east

it tells me to burrow in the dirt,

leave my clothes on the edge

of graves self-made

leave here, leave now—

I am a fragile thing, a small child
crying for voice, hearing nothing
as my own constricts

I am the hand, the dying light,
the cry fading in the dark

I wonder if there
will ever be a
reprieve
solace,
somewhere

I wonder if there
will ever be a
reprieve
solace,
somewhere

FADE INTO MIDDLE AGE

sundays are for lovers,

for you & I,

for grocery shopping,

you have wine,

I have an edible

we clean the

house of things

we don't need, garage sales

& bin bound

I clean my bike as if I will ride it,

& you smile as I stumble

on the pavement,

as if you believe me

sundays are for lovers

you prepare meat for the grill,

& I pretend I'll like it

corn on the cob

& the breeze is like spring,

like opening up a door

to who we were

sundays are for us,

& as we fade into middle age,

I do not mourn the wasted

ways we drifted

RATTLE IN MY MARROW

it takes, you know?

this world we spin on,

the terrors are long,

the nights are dizzy—

a blur

where goes

the work done?

the friendships

about to blossom?

no gentle laugh

around table,

no soft hand

upon shoulder

who holds me

but the counting?

who holds me

but the obsession?

when the medicine dries up,

who do I become

when nothing

can hide this rattle

in my marrow?

SPIDER LEGS

a silent entity—
always with me
under the surface,
living & breathing
like the monster it is

the monster I know,
but hold hands with,
so we die together

a fire breathing thing
a focus stealing thing

a monster with no name,
new eyes, & a mouth
using me to destroy
the world around me

has this always been me?

the mirror doesn't know,

can't check this pulse,

can't read the charts

she can stare,

look deep into iris,

map the quiver of lip

& steering of brow

what matter is this mind,

brimming, boiling—

begging to be

put to sleep,

to erase the day

did he look at you funny?

the stranger in the store

must know,

must see the delicate walls

spider legs

crawl fast, fall faint

under the surface—

living & breathing

like the monster it is

YOUR QUEEN OF BROKEN HEARTS

a tan dog on a dirty carpet,

some kid is screaming in the street,

& we are childless,

barren, broken open

with a smile we hide

the movie we watched last night

didn't hit us the right way,

& I find fault with your criticisms,

& spout my own

you're not like the mold,

far from perfect,

& I am a live wire,

a bear trap you

avoid on odd days

I am turning in the wind,

ready to fly away in the past

& anchored to

you here in this present

your queen of broken hearts

your queen of the split mind

& the lazy start to summers

when you beg me to devour sunshine

I am always
tumbling into
familiar holes

until then, I shall
fall + fall
+ fall
again

IT LOSES GRACE

it's starts simply—
one little buzzing bee,
circling carefully around
my manic mind

I let it in
I always let it in

it bounces around
landing softly,
velvety,
on the edges

it's silent—
it's quite quiet

but I always hear
the whisper in the wind,

& when I do,

it becomes wide

eyed & frantic

it picks up pace

it loses grace

I'm dazed & dizzy

chasing this erratic thief

always stealing my sanity

always filling me

with anxious anguish

SKIN WALKER

I am the phantom,
too long pressed
against the fabric of
the cave inside of me

I fell down a dark hole,
broken nails
casualties
of the descent

my one friend
a broken clock
right once or twice
about the moments
lost when the dark kisses
me slowly

I am the phantom,

the ill intent breeding

behind closed eyes

I am not her,

this skin walker,

this voiceless

being peering

over my shoulders,

steering my life

like a runaway carjacker

THE KINDNESS OF OUR YOUTH

who is the one

with the knife?

silent killer,

empty smile

the venom falls

from lips to fingers,

from screen to eyes

how far we've fallen

from the kindness of our youth,

how shocking our

words must sound

broken glass,

shattered kindness

how does this world feel

to those with

overwhelmed hearts?

can they see the

shadow in the room?

the venom falls

from lips to temples,

from stranger to stranger

knife tucked neatly

in smiles & masks,

hand in hand

HEART LIKE A VICE

lips sewn

shut like

a doll in an

antique store,

I am no novelty,

no faded cloth

my lungs pull in air

& beg for solace

I am no dress-up being,

no lifeless toy

lips sewn shut,

earthquake rumble

head like a balloon,

heart like a vice

ENJOY THE RIDE

sometimes I think

you're possessed

your clap happy jaw

never stays shut

a thief in the night

stole my smile,

but he tightened yours on,

slapped your ass—

enjoy the ride

he tossed it

over his shoulder

as he descended the white

shutters & hit

the ground running

sometimes

I think he slipped

a song behind your ear

left it there for

me to stare down hard,

long mirror

I can never live up to

sometimes I think

I'm possessed

I'm doing better today
I bought groceries
I cooked those groceries
I rinsed the dishes in the sink when I
was done
cooking those groceries
I ate organic because something
inside of me is sick;
I think I drank a glass of water
with my dinner

I'm doing better today

DEVOUR THE AIR

I want to tell you

about the longing in my bones

the way it

whimpers in the night

the way it keeps me up,

whispering for you

there is a reaching

that races

beneath my skin—

when the world quiets,

when the sun is in slumber

I try to keep up

with the river there,

I try to devour the air that

hasn't touched your skin in years

I try to ride the current

that doesn't feel like

your current, your touch

I want to tell you

about the longing

in my veins

I want to tell you—

come back to me

so that I can tell you

WHAT A SHOW TO WATCH

the picture show

shows me life,

warm smiles, hearty laugh

I am not here,

I am no love—

I am hands to the screen,

cupping the light,

inhaling the scent of life

unlived

my palm rustles dust,

streaks grey,

the picture show shows

me my body,

unmarred,

& I pull down

these smudged

glasses,

take out the red pen

there is a scar here;

I know it

I'll find it

the tests lie to me,

& I am a line in the dark,

a red mark

you cannot cross over

the picture show

shows me wide smiles,

a rollercoaster on a hot day,

& I am weary

of the one in my mind

the picture show

shows me they

cannot hurt like *me*;

what a lie to devour,

what a show to watch

CROWD OF BLACK EYES

the crow on my shoulder

is a beauty—

black like the caverns

of my mind

he is a fortune teller,

a crowded crowd

of black eyes

he tells me the wrist

will break,

the boulder will fall

I am weak as the

weakness I breed

there is a seer,

a judge,

a close-knit friend

to my false lines

the crow on my shoulder

is a beauty—

a mirror to my own mind

INSISTENCE

maybe I'll crumble

under the bricks

placed upon me

no sabbatical—

no new year of wonder

I'm just wondering

how to survive this

when I'll be free to worry

about the shadows

stuck

in the corners of my heart

I know I'm not alone

silver linings, they say

but god, this terror

when it wraps around me

I sometimes choke

did you know

I'm one of the lucky ones?

I wish I could remember

my mind's insistence—

six feet under

where is the truth?

I'm supposed to bleed
to make my
writing real &
raw & what it
should be for you

TRAGIC & WARM

there is sunlight in our bedroom,

& your face is perfect,

round & the stubble I feel

as I rustle you reminds

me that men like you are magic,

& warm

you untangle me,

& my manic moments

you are the balm,

the constant,

the cure for the ailments

I used to drown, but

there is sunlight in

our bedroom

as you sleep beside me

WALLPAPER LIFE

what do I need but this?

the walls do not laugh

when I push by,

the shades

do not laugh as I break free

I am better at alone,

at the walls you say cage me—

lie & say you need me,

lie & say I am more

than a space filler,

a hand on a cold drink,

I am better at this

wallpaper life,

cosmic wandering

where no one can

let eyes linger

I am better at

believing the lie,

seeing the phantom

hand closing my door

I am better at alone,

because their eyes scare me

THREE TIMES, LOVER

check the lock

twice, lover

I'm sorry for being this way—

for trying this way—

will the fire burn us?

money waves &

strangers cave to

baser instincts

check the lock

three times, lover

I'm sorry the clock

in my head wins,

the math they

don't teach in school

check the door,

lover?

was that a knock I heard?

MARRIED MOMENT

when I close my eyes,

I see the blood,

the bathtub,

& your vibrant wounds

why did you look to

me to find you?

why did you believe

I could stitch wounds that deep?

I can't drive to a new street;

the houses all look like

the one we shared;

I'm afraid I'll drive up,

open the door,

see you on the brink

of the unknown

when I close my eyes,

I can hear the buzzing,

your call to me &

the guilt lodged in my throat

when I close my eyes,

I can hear the silence,

the unanswered texts,

& the married moment

before my eyes took it in

I am still scared of/for you

I always feel the
need to hide
my wounds

SMOKING GUN

was this what

you signed up for?

defiant rage,

no bubbling brook

as we walk the line,

but a bubbling woman

tied to her insecurities,

situations manifested into

burnt bile in her belly

& tears shed in the grey

you signed your name

on the line & signed up as

lover, caregiver,

kisser of knees & made

up stories

I hide from

you are a gentle hum,

a comforting snore in the night

you are constant & steady

soft skin & the

only person

I can spend every

waking hour with

your manic queen,

your undoing

the nightmare you

cannot wake from

I wonder what

comfort I bring,

if it's only in my

reliable stumbles,

my grappling

for the lifeline,

threadbare & wavering

was this what

you signed up for?

a ghost of a woman hell

bent on ruining her own day,

yours a casualty

I love you,

it is my smoking gun

DO NOT LEAVE THIS WORLD
WITHOUT TELLING ME GOODBYE

I would swim the oceans for you,

for the touch of your hand,

for the feel of your arms around me,

a hug to ease this ache

nearly a thousand days,

& I cannot dull this pain,

this worry

do not leave this world

without touching my brow,

do not leave this world

without telling me goodbye

I would swim the oceans for you

I can erase the crimson
quickly

TRYING TO BE WHAT HE DESERVES

softly,

never turning my way

I pull myself from my self—

the place I linger too often

I reach across the leather sea

& touch his hairline

he sighs,

&

sinks

he needs me

& I am trying,

trying to be what he deserves

WHERE IS THE APPLAUSE?

where is the crown?

there is no slow clap

for this waking,

this venture to

the other side

I cannot leave behind endless

nights warring in my mind

my words cannot falter,

I am this voice,

this opening-up

I cannot give in to

the numbness;

the words lodged

in my throat

I cannot leave behind

clasped hands,

this mania skipping along

my spine like pavement,

the hopscotch of years past—

where is the applause?

CASTLE OF MY OWN

I don't know

where we go from here

what terror

what horror

will I ever be okay?

I beg it out loud,

look twice in the mirror

try the words out on a whisper,

type out a status

erase it three times

is it just me?

is the castle my own?

what horror,

false honesty,

the door is shut

& the world still gets in

false security & hope
hold me too close,
& I'm falling awake in
gentle rumbles

where will I go from here?

I like to flaunt a fantasy
& hope that
you'll search for
my essence
in every manic letter

READY THE GUILLOTINE

I've had three glasses

of wine in two

& a half years

the grip—

the anxiety liquid fire

brought me has dulled,

& I hide away from the is reality—

shackled to the chains of eyes

I invited into my abstinence

I finally started medicating

myself with weed,

& I have never felt a

warm coat like this,

a shield to my mind,

warring in-between my eyes,

begging for a prize

I am multifaceted,

& society says

we are paper-thin,

good & bad,

no in-between

we will fracture under this weight—

this stealing microphone

strapped to our palms,

begging for a word,

any word,

so we can ready the guillotine

BROKEN CHESS PIECES

voiceless demon
in the corner,
eyes like night,
smile spread thin
like a threat

the witching hour
is our meeting,
our special prison

the blame is left wanting
like a one-night stand

where am I if not here?
if not in perpetual
waiting for this time,
this breath of choking air

I am falling,

broken chess pieces,

& I'm bored with

the way this board

pulls me across its surface

my heartbeat was here once,
red ribbon is all that's left

THE SOUND OF PEACE

you are the sound of peace,

the cure for long days

when I can run

my fingers on your back

hear your gentle snore,

nudge you when it gets too loud

you are strong legs tangled with mine

beneath the covers

you are the sound of peace

WARM FROM THE HUNT

hungry mouth, open throat,

you wait for me to step in,

to offer shy smile

demon captor,

demon voice,

you call to me in

dark nights,

in waking days,

you are sleepless,

timeless,

I spend less time

in the new *new* freshness

of a warm shower,

of a sleepy smile

I am ever waiting for you,

hungry mouth,

eyelash on cheek

demon captor, I
am restless of
fighting with you,

warm from the hunt,
warm from the day
walking descent into the fire

I could sleep for days;
I could fall into
this potent pull

WHAT DO I SAY IN THE DARK?

I see it flickering—

dry throat

numb limbs

how do I run from a faceless terror?

is my house a refuge

or a space for my fears to breed

in my heavy center?

abyss—

I fall

useless & tumbling

I see it flickering

a future

solid once,

never promised

grief is a flameless fire

grief is ash in my belly

I taste nothing else

where do I look?

what do I say in the dark?

when I was younger
I could list all of the things
I knew I needed to be happy

+ I was convinced once I
had them in my hands, life would
be perfect
—a two-story house
—a car that didn't break down all the time
—weekends off
—someone who loves me unconditionally

now I have all of that,
+ I can't figure out
why I still get
sad from time to time

HEAVY IS MY NEED FOR YOU

heavy is this grey burden—

open cage,

violet confession

I cannot stay here

I miss you,

long for your bed

the calm of you—

the smile & laugh

to live here

is to die slowly

open windows,

no peace

the flood is neat

never-ending,

lucid drowning,

slow water in my ears

heavy is the air—

rich is my need for you

when the world crumbles,

heavy is the grey

fading burden

they say we will

not carry for long

STARVING MINUTIA

dripping faucet,

why do you taunt?

why do you smile

while driving me mad?

there's a car crash

on the tip of my tongue;

I cannot speak

it into existence,

I cannot give way

to the premonitions,

the starving minutia

of these waking dreams

dripping fact;

why do you torment?

I am raindrops

on canvas on good days,

torrential flood on dark nights

I live there, on sheets,

soft plea to make

the voices stop

as dreams caress others

I don't know how to

outrun this never-ending lie

UNTIL YOU DIDN'T

through cold winter's edge,

& the expanse of my heart—

be here—stay here—love here…it beats

you lived there,

in the fringes of us,

of what we could be

walked with an

open palm,

holding my timid fingers

& my eyes closed,

the glow of you

bringing me out,

over & over

& over again

bringing my smile

& my laugh,

my fragile warmth

you loved here,

in the bitter,

in the desolate nights

until you didn't…

until warmer shores

brought calls you

could not ignore

my eyes closed

& I can still hear you,

your three-letter phrase

& your dawn-like voice

through cold, winter's edge,

& the expanse of my heart—

come back—stay here—

live with me here…it calls

the worst part is
when I try to uncomplicate
myself to make
everyone around me feel 'comfortable'

don't mind the freak over here
she has many talents,
one is pretending to be
vanilla sweetness just like you

I am so tired of bending & breaking
I am so tired of apologizing
with my eyes,
with my words,
for the flesh & bone
woman that I am

LOST LIGHT ON MY EYELASHES

spinning wheel,

we are lost here—

to-do lists in a pile,

lost light on my eyelashes

I cannot feel the breath,

cannot feel the slow drift

cannot obsess

on anything

but the gnawing weight,

the hollow heart

A BEGGAR AMONG THIEVES

& how high

will the waves reach?

I am drowning, clawing,

a sea-witch among liars

you cannot catch me,

I will go to depths unheard of,

the dark is a lover

I long to divorce,

pull close in the night

I am salt,

open gullet to tears I purge

& how low can I dive?

I am descending,

pretending I'm okay

in the light of day

as the birds call my

name overhead,

echoes of a dying light

I am drowning,

clawing,

a beggar among thieves

LIGHT DIES

I can hear their laughter,

manifested in my own dreams,

my own violet & red

& fire thoughts

the bull in the corner

of the room has hot

breath & black eyes

I am the bullseye,

the feeding break

the moment we

take a slow blink,

pretend it'll

never happen to us

we are not schoolchildren

anymore;

we are beyond this, right?

I can hear the laughter

manifested in my own dreams,

my own memories

light dies on

their assumptions,

on the criticisms

their tongue laps

I can hear their laughter

SOMETIMES THINGS GET
REALLY BAD

you are frozen

& the dishes pile up

& you start the dryer to

get the

wrinkles out,

knowing you'll have

to start it again

you feed the dogs,

but don't feed yourself

(a solace there)

you stay up until 2am

with the mania,

searching for old

messages from almost-lovers,

& ones you *had* but lost

(a solace there)

you ignore the journal,

though you know it will help

you drink caffeine,

though you know it won't help

you don't do yoga,

knowing it will help

you take two sleeping

pills & count to seventy-three

in the dark of your room, alone

you sleep with a knife

under your pillow

because the moonlight

man could be one door over

sometimes things get really bad

the house plants wilt with me,
silent friends in my dissolve

TRANSGRESSIONS

it's a ticking, a slow crawl,

I can hear the chime before it's time

I am a mouth full of sand,

a pocket fill of wants

where is my time?

a red mark on my heart,

a day spent up, washed away

I am counting in my head again,

transgressions against my list to-do,

impressions of a woman

with a life in line with all

her dreams & wonderings

it's a ticking, a slow roll to the finale,

the adieu, the curtain call

I will never be ready for

I can hear my sigh before it's time

WHEN THE LAST PETAL HAS FALLEN

there is strength in your bones,

even when others see fit to

break them down

there is a humming in your heart

& I can hear it from here

your story traveled miles to

my crying eyes & humbled heart

what do you lose in the giving?

what do you gain?

when the last petal has fallen

we will know what you've done,

who you've cared for

those tears you shed,

water more

than you know

we forgive the salt

we feel the healing

there is strength in your bones,

there is a humming in the

way you long to lift

everyone you touch can feel it

I WOULD BE LIKE EVERYONE ELSE

it would've been easy

it would've been acceptable

it would've been the return

of the laughter

it would've been the return of the me

I used to be

it would've been the return of chaos

I could've done it easily

three drinks

& I would be like everyone else

happy, laughing

I would be like everyone else

I would lose who I am to it

I would become the monster

become the jester

become the executioner

I would become who I was

who they long for me to be again

because they can't see the guillotine

they don't know I am on the table

I am lowering the rope

I am in charge of the blade

I want to sit on the front porch
+ hear the birds,
the neighbors on their lawn
the distant sound of a dog barking

I want to sit on the front porch,
+ escape this modern world

TIME HAS NO KINGDOM HERE

sleep,

hold me close

whisper your slow song to me

is it the dark I crave?

the moonlight man,

& the way his deep voice

tells me this is brave—

this is where I belong

time has no kingdom here

father clock is cold & nameless

their faces,

they blur

round & round

four times too many

sleep,

hold me close

this false reality cannot have me

PAPER-THIN LIE

did the veil lift?

soft focus,

harsh words,

high aim

stoop low,

muddled brain,

negligence

wide eyes

& you're paper-thin

someone I could rip

from my life

do I want to kiss

goodbyes into the wind?

I cannot hold you

instead, I hold onto

the *you* I thought you were

this thin veil

so delicate in shading

so revealing of who I am,

who I want to be—

how they misalign

I am so terrified

of this paper-thin lie

GRENADES ON YOUR TONGUE

& now,

they want me silenced

they want me quiet, meek

they want me to swallow

these grenades on my tongue

they forget that

my past is my past, I own it

I own their part in it

& I own the pain

they've inflicted

I own the stories sitting hot

inside this chest

reach, reach all you want,

they are buried too deep

for you to touch

how many seasons of this life
do I have to live
until I am nothing more
than a caricature of my former self?

A PAINTING IN VENGEANCE

my anger is like a

feral dog in my belly

scratching to get out,

& I am too stubborn &

blind to listen to caged animals

in my possession

I had a painting made last

week depicting the way I

used to be

sometimes it vaults

off the wall & tries to run

away but I have not let myself

have my way in years

I told the artist not to color

my face in vengeance, but in love,

the kind I used to carry in my

cupped hands, when

I was soft & caged myself

when the lighting is right, I can

see contempt lingering

on my bottom lip,

& just like before,

I do not

say a word,

I just roll over &

close my eyes

offering myself

unforgiveness instead

SCORCHING SKIN

make way for

the voices,

they speak to me—

their slithering seduction

rolls off my scorching skin

make way

for the marring,

the scarring,

the brutal beatings

I lay upon myself

make way for

ruining hands,

make way for

my raging heart

make way for my

deafening silence,

only I can exist here,

only I can survive

myself

SPAT ME OUT

the world opened
her mouth,
bared her teeth,
swallowed me whole

said she wanted me to feel
the sadness inside her

said she wanted to
marry it
to the melancholy
in my marrow

said sorrow stings,
I tasted of borrowed bitter,
spat me out, made me
into something new

I wanted to live inside

that belly

I wanted to burn inside

that belly

I am fragments & red
an ache in the skin between
my breasts

BREAK OVER YOU

you're a man—

you're a lighthouse,

you live in the

eye of the storm,

chained to the sea

that is me

it is no burden, but

a blessing to let the

crash of my waves

break over you

how do we give thanks

to those who create calm

where our

kiss meets the shore?

everything I didn't

know I needed

lives in the body

of you

your light does not dim,

it takes all of me in

this life we have created

was unmapped, unwritten

in my plans,

this life we have

is our own &

no one can take it away

SHEDDING OF SELF

in the dark comes the birth—

night flowers blooming

when the world crumbles apart

you were made for this,

this cracking open,

this deep & torturous

shedding of self

the dark comes, & you

tilt the mirror, find yourself

in the shadows of the room

the grey hands

cannot hold you down,

you place your feet upon them,

stepping stones to

the open air

to the life waiting in the

corners of your mind,

that you will manifest

blue & blinding

& beautifully dark

in the dark comes the birth—

the labor transcendent,

the new you that you are,

never again to be

silenced once more

THOUGH I LONG FOR YOU TO BE

soft wail in the distance;

you cannot find me here

limp wrist, eyes buried in

bright bring light

& faraway worlds

this is not peace,

not mother's milk

this is not therapy or healing

this is an echo,

& I am a dark cry

soft wail in the distance,

you are not her voice,

though I long for you to be

I will avoid your eye,

the slam of the door,

the gurney,

the press *press* to

my wildly alive chest

I AM HERE IN THE NOW

in the shadows,

with the low melody,

the slow & delicate

beat of this life

I am here in the pale

white glow,

in the shattered glass,

& the open hands

this heart is beating,

blinding, shaking hands

with the images of

strangers in my dreams

who will be lovers

in my future

I am here in the now—

in the waning & glowing
of each passing day

in the shedding of layers
& past days
that made me this person
I see smiling back
from the mirror

I am here in the
colors of dawn,
in the whisper of dusk

I am here in this life
I have built,
& I live it with a lust
for the waking

THE WOUND IS OF FLESH

red & blinding,

piercing protection & armor

the wound is of steel—

breaking & rust spilling

but you, you are not of flesh

you are more than bone

oh, you,

you are more than of

this earth

bright mind & blue spirit

bright smile & unforgotten

tenacity

this is not ending,

not altering the strength inside

oh, you,

of this life,

of this choice to

endure when the sun shines

on you again

the wound is of flesh,

the healing is of heart

you are piercing & armor that

cannot—will not—be worn

to the breaking

laugh spilling,

rust rejoicing

you are stronger

than you know

ACKNOWLEDGMENTS

Thank you to everyone who shared their struggles with anxiety with me: Cyndy, Alexandra S, Tiffany Stells, Tiffany, Chèri-lee Fisher, Emily, Trisha, Jaylynn, Haylee, Cassandra, Anna lisa Vitale, Leila, Burgundy, Jocelyn, Leeah Fisher, Amy Murdock, Sara Kessack, Leah Mangold

J.R. Rogue first put pen to paper at fifteen after developing an unrequited high school crush and has never stopped writing about heartache. She has published multiple volumes of poetry and novels. Her work has been recognized with three Goodreads Choice Awards nominations, a testament to the impact of her work on readers.

In addition to her writing, J.R. Rogue is a certified yoga teacher with additional certification in Yoga Nidra and Trauma-Informed Yoga. She is passionate about mindfulness and meditation and is studying Foundations in Meditation. Furthermore, J.R. Rogue has been sober from alcohol since January 1st, 2020, a personal achievement that she is proud of and that has strengthened her commitment to mindfulness and wellness.

J.R. Rogue resides in a small town in the Midwest with her family, where she enjoys a peaceful life reading and telling stories.

You can find important links and information here. Join her mailing list to keep up with everything she's working on.

www.jrrogue.com
contact@jrrogue.com

instagram.com/authorjrrogue
threads.net/@j.r.rogue
facebook.com/jrrogueauthor
tiktok.com/@jenro501
amazon.com/J.-R.-Rogue
bookbub.com/authors/j-r-rogue
pinterest.com/rogueauthor

ALSO BY J. R. ROGUE

Romance

MUSE & MUSIC SERIES

Breaking Mercy

Burning Muses

Background Music

Blind Melody

SOMETHING LIKE LOVE SERIES

I Like You, I Love Her

I Love You, I Need Him

I Like You, I Hate Her

Romantic Suspense

RED NOTE SERIES

The Rebound

The Regret

The Return

Supernatural Suspense

OZARK OMENS SERIES

The Girl Next Door

STANDALONE NOVELS

Kiss Me Like You Mean It

9 798224 899951